New

James Bertolino

New

& Selected Poems

Carnegie-Mellon University Press
Pittsburgh & London 1978

For Lois

Acknowledgments

Grateful acknowledgement is made to the following
magazines and anthologies where many of these poems
have appeared:

*Abraxas, Apple, Ark River Review, Choice, Cincinnati
Poetry Review, Cold Duck, Cottonwood Review, The
Dragonfly, Epoch, The Florida Quarterly, Foxfire,
The Goodly Co., Hearse, Heartland II Poets of the
Midwest (Northern Illinois University Press), Lillabulero,
Minnesota Review, The New Salt Creek Reader, Northwest
Review, Ox Head 8, The Painted Bride Quarterly, Paris
Review, Partisan Review, Poems One Line or Longer
(Grossman), Poetry, The Poetry Bag, Red Cedar Review,
Road Apple Review, The Small Pond, Spring Rain,
Stinktree, Three Rivers Poetry Journal, Trace, Waters,
West Coast Review and Wisconsin Review.*

The "Selected" poems in this volume are reprinted
from EMPLOYED, 1972, Ithaca House; SOFT ROCK, 1973,
Charas Press; and THE GESTURES, 1975, Bonewhistle Press.

Published with the help of the Charles Phelps Taft
Memorial Fund, University of Cincinnati.

Distributed by
University of Pittsburgh Press
127 N. Bellefield Avenue
Pittsburgh, Pennsylvania 15260

CONTENTS

THREE New Poems

I Think of Roethke

I think of Roethke's
raging greenhouse
perfecting sun

& flower dumps

when I want so bad
for this tight bud
to explode
on the page.

The Red Dress

The whirr
of the sewing machine

her back
    bent
beautiful in the tension
of her toil

the purr
of my thread
    between
her fingers

brings her to me,
brings us,
weaves me in the house
of her

& nowhere
is there stronger
more soft
    fabric
than this

The Night Was Smooth

Sure the night was smooth
as milkweed silk
against the fingers,
& the wet rags just washed
were warm;
even the doctor's rough farm hands
had knowing, were good.
There was a confidence.

But the baby wasn't right.

Elegy

1.

Old Growley died this year.
They pushed his
rotten wood trailer
over the rim of the dump
where he presided
as long as I can remember.
The men took Squeaks,
his grim little dog,
away too.

2.

A bent woman
who itched her chin
on her knee
as she walked, & slept
on the cold Courthouse steps
(except in winter . . . I don't know where
she slept then),
doesn't feed the pigeons
anymore &
they've flown to the park
where musty old men
attempt to fool them
with cigar-butts.

3.

A green Mack truck
(with no trailer)
bore down upon a preoccupied
wren,
& before the feathers
had settled
three sparrows &
the rest
of the wrens
were singing again.

Memorial Park at Sunrise

On the damp grass
a sandwich
in a greasy brown bag

salami on dry rye
tired frills of lettuce
along its edge

creating a gentle resonance

with the snuffling
of the wino
on the bench

adrift in a dream of wheatfields
& sunlight

under a shifting paper canopy

of yesterday's
crime.

Employed

I quit my job this morning.

They couldn't understand
ducks
rippling across my mind
from shore to weeds & back
or down for grub.

What's more I didn't care
for their caring to keep me
behind a counter. Blue

moving into green on the hills
& the black snake
with red stripes the length of its body

stretch my eyes
beyond books

tell me I'm right,
I'm right.

As If Bound

In a field
the summer grass thick
& short
slope stubbled grey
with boulders
some larger than
the roofs of old cars

you notice
the birds
whether alone or in flocks
coming over
              dip
with the hill

your own eyesight seems
to bow towards
those boulders
when you would look beyond
to the fine oaks
near the creek

& is it perhaps
that they alone have gone
the distance you
are the first mile of

that they in their cool shapes
hold everything's
right name?

Beyond the Storm

The storm has come again today,
it rages shrill pins.
I hear a pale child
moaning alone
by the bottom rocks of the field.
I feel the blowing wet
bruise her face.

Three days have been
since Marlys left
in her wool coat, winding
down the fright of the path, dark.
The branches are knives.
Out of lulling wind comes quacking,
a duck on the raft.

I can't remember how long
the fire's been cooled,
& my legs are twitching more today.
Stomach too moans more than hunger;
I'm afraid.

Lying here the shadows make shapes
with my hand. The storm
is subsiding. There's a cricket
under the bed.

Day of Change

My name is June
Bug. I feel splitting

bamboo when the wind
hits. My legs cannot

smooth to the flight
of birds. I want soon

for this chamber
to pass. I need the length

of the snake. I have
seen so much.

Portrait: My American Man
Fall, 1967

Sweat beads the fuzz
on my nose.
I feel pimples swell.
In the booth
behind my ears
a young girl with no pants
hawks
her dream. Dust
from her mother's petticoats
chokes
the light.

I have strong need.
Visions
have passed me by.
I can't write poetry, but my wife
is negro
      & nightly
the same green centipede
wades
into my sleep.

Love's Body Consumed

Out beyond
unused skins &
rows
of bed-springs rusting

on plains of ice

lay naked sons
mouths
quaking no blood sound.

Fingers locked
angels
& underworld beasts
rut
their circle tighter

perform unholy
more
than circumcision

cleave
& carry off

to bronze clicking
to his mandible
they dance

the Father feeding.

She Dreams the Pelvis

Shackled

her wail
a stairway
circling down
the dream

her flesh
spittle-flecked
shimmers

& the pelvis

out of control
plunges

between white thighs
locked
the bannister slicks

a razor

The Veteran

A dry sense of dread
keeps him in bed
not going to work
not shaving
not watering the begonias

now slim crawling light
                          he's sure
they hive,
            spiders
in a crack
near his pillow,
near his ears

wonders
what he's harbored
what poisons
for years / & god he's frightened
of the raking sun!

    this fourth-year sun
    off the fat pink belly
    of a puppy he drowned

        his sister's
        fat puppy
        belly-up
        in a pond

The Baker

The Baker
fascinated by a dream
of sea-horses
awoke late

Unkneaded
the sourdough sprouted
yellow pods
took to the air

Entering the shop
the last bits of his life
flashed by
in the jaws of hornets
smelling of mold

I Sold a Poem

You turn from me.

It's just
a normal night, we did
run out of ice,
& just perhaps
it was the trash I meant
but then forgot
to dump. I kissed your nose
the way I always do.
I agreed I should
have come home sooner. You know
I sold a poem;
you said you understood.
I would have
called
but my mouth was cold with beer.

It's no big thing.

I'm near you now & you concede
that certain times
in certain ways
I must be free.

You understand.
I understand.
                    But god,

tonight you turn from me.

The Marriage

I am a turtle
with a lead shell,
with fragile blue wings
of gossamer
& small.
The sky is far
when you say you're though.

You are a bobcat
with thin claws of glass,
with grey dreamy eyes
of no luster.
The green tall trees
are emery
when I say I don't love you.

Night comes.
The air is sparse,
the ground cold.
Our eyes round owls
afraid in the dark.
Give my hour hand,
it will hold us.

Barefoot Lover

This morning
a loaded moving-van bound west
crushed
the apricot pits
you spit
to my street
while strolling with your lover
last night

How they burn my feet

Notes for an Elegy

How much easier
   at my window
to be without passion
now winter has come

& the dreadful need
that pushed me late madly to dance
is cold.

Wind shifts grey
without pleasure
in the oaks.

The moon climbs
weary & desperate this design
out of the brush
near the J. Ville Creek.

Snow Angel

Outside my window
a small girl staggers
with the weight
of a hunk of snow. Now
she is breaking it
against a tree. My hands
are cold.

Outside the window
the same girl now
is on her back, she moves
first one leg then
the other, first one arm
then all at once
an angel!

There are angels covering
the lawn. Where their thighs
divide
the green grass pushes
for sun. My winter
is melting. Pieces of angels
break against my limbs.

Yellow Spring

Everything outside
is yellow. A crater
in the sidewalk
left by the come
& go of Winter, daily
fills up with
popsicle sticks.
When she passes
the air this side my window
crackles, everything, the empty
bread-box has a red edge.
This color is me.
She smiles into the sun
above the house.
She is innocent. I want
fiercely
to touch her.

The Blood Vision

On the dusty bare boards
of this shack
this simple rotting lean-to
where the angles

of my limbs
tangle with
the churning furred sticks
of my dog

I sense his dream
stretching
the dark space above my eyes

& feel I want to step
through
his skin

to taste the warm blood
of a quail's pumping
between my jaws

Changes

This is the
moment

with care
the pennies laid
the three of them
a triangle
on lake ice

a time of
waiting

months
they've settled
drove
their own clear shafts

through

one   now the
three
of them   free
in the currents

changing this
moment

your life.

Blue Bottle

Lightning
cleaves
wet foilage

a bottle
buried
with its mouth open to the air
fuses

in the instant's heat

captures in
molten glass
the solitary dung beetle
seduced

deep

by the bottle's
thick
sugared water

now a halo
of white crystals/
                    orbits
about this dark form
suspended

forever

a dead star

In Liquid Moonlight

I watch a snail
swim slowly
its clear glue

over the length of a blade of grass

& the blade, flattened
in a glistening bond

shudders

begins to bow upwards
pulling
the elastic clear muscle
to a single strand
of light

which vibrates

the lucid
single
thought

of snail

Spring Thaw: Fish

Now with the first
trickle
about frozen gills

the images

the long secret

the endless strange rope
whispering
through the cold scaled form

speeds up, images
blur
the friction

pulls
the body begins
to move

in the currents
free

dumbly

of the slow
clarity
of ice

The Scavenge

For Jennifer

A certain neccessity
for clamshells.
Simple beach-dirtied clamshells.

Her brown calves knot
below the rough-weave shift
as she bends

to pick through the pebbles
& black twigs
for the clamshells.

The bits of clam flesh
still clung to slick inner walls
do not matter. Tiny clots

of plankton & crushed kelp,
barnacles even
pass with all

through the mouth of her sack.

Now back at the driftwood lean-to
the salt water soup
boils them clean, clean enough

to be ladled from the pot, wind-dried
& strung
about her moist bronze flesh

to catch the sun.

On a Line by John Ashbery

The space was
magnificent & dry.
You slid your

cold hands up
beneath my sweater
whispering "I love

your body" to my ear
that I not be surprised
by the chill. Your chin

resting on my shoulder.
Together we watched
a lone gull bring down

the sun. An abrupt
shrill cry. Somewhere
off along the beach

the small life
of a bird or chipmunk
was complete.

The Gulls

She stands in the shadow
of the cliffs,
her eyes holding
the sea's last glow.
As I pass
she turns slowly,
dark hair sifting
the salt air. I reach out
as if to draw from her darkening mouth
the smile,
      But no,
her eyes close to the wind.
Only the gulls
lifting & falling
over the sand.
Only her whisper: *Yes*

I know you. I am
your widow.

Lizard

Stopped and awful as a photograph
of somebody laughing,
But ten years dead.
—Sylvia Plath

It was you in the photo
the one Jamesy took
that blithe day
at the beach. The moment after
I think
when you held the gull's bones
in the salt spray above your head
for us to see—the rib-caught leaves
tiny flags flapping
on their tethers.

"I thought it was a lizard," you said.
"Alive!"
      & laughed
into the still freeze
of a photograph,
your long red hair still ruffled
by the scream.

39

After the Climb

Her mouth
embraces

the last clear column of air
poised
on the hill

For a moment
the cleft root
of her throat
glows

as the weeds grow familiar
& pull her down

I Had a Packard

The last fluorescent lamp-post
in the parking lot
blinked, sputtered &
went out
       that we might learn joy.

Whose time paid
that our fuse
be blown?
       I worked

the damp night

through the back door
under the fall elm
to the wet sparkling lot
behind the A&P.
       In that cool air

our pleasure hovers still.

The Story

Between long fingers
nails glowing
delicate the ash bends slowly towards
her sleek leg
the fine dark mesh
with a reflection
shifting
as she breathes

          she listens

to his story
intent on
the details, the names
of the women
the way his clever hands
lithe animals
dived
to surface with her pain

Song for the Unborn

Her cunt invents
his mouth

Through these lips pass
like small
tongues
the names
of their children

The Cold Room

Because we kept no belief

Because hunger

You reach to close my rough fingers over
a knocking at the heart

The oak table
blasphemes
the name we called love

& the walls collect
like stricken
petals
our failing breath

Relentless

In the wall
she sees
revolving
the flowers of her life

black-eyed susans
& tiger lilies

her patient mind
notes them today
by name

A lizard
deep
in the greenery
breathes

a shadow
deadly
to the careful resonance

cancer

in this gentle
delusion
her revolving
flowers of the wall

Something Familiar

You are 83 years old
& the car you are driving
is an island
that everywhere leans
toward you

there are no birds
but the air is full
a tepid bath
about your limbs

you think you have been sleeping
& wonder slowly
if you have missed
a favorite cast of sun through leaves
or a face

it's your neighborhood
you've been passing, & here
someone would know you
some hand might wave
from the haze

you go slowly, & it's warm
& you're sure there is someone

but you can't remember who

The Flower

Each petal of grief grows
limp and falls, the
irresistible music of its turning
slips through us
& we tremble,
believing only now in un-
earthly flowers
that live not by water but
heave to life with our blood.

Talisman

From the musty bed his out-
stretched toes could touch
the brick holding the room's
chill center. Speak

to me speak you wall you
dirty sink. The room infested
with books, bad company
all of them. He knew their names

they responded never &
now printed paper, garbage
sink & brick, the walls
& floor slid the chute of

his consciousness to the empty
the unplugged & ringing snail
shell on the windowsill I'm
here I'm here I love you Jim.

The Landscape

I draw a line from
edge to edge
to provide place, a land-

scape within which
to begin. Birds

float down from a great height
across the page, wings
like paper kites

brushing air, eyes
flashing the
landing lights

of the 747
gear unfolding seat-
belt warning holds

our attention the squeek
stomachs clutching
as cement grabs rubber

you touch my hand it's
been nice Jim maybe we'll run

into each other someplace honey.

Selecting a Reader
after Kooser

First, I would have her
be you. Not beautiful
really, not like anyone.
You feel good about women.
Riding the elevator with six
or seven, you aren't
uncomfortable with the young black.
"I think this will be a good day"
makes them all feel they know you
in this the hotel where they live.
The blouse you are wearing is loose
& fashionable, & it's
been washed. You're someone
whose arm we might touch.
You know that it is Spring outside
& in the way that's
yours, we know we'll live,
we'll be okay.

Snowblind

Use a word like
slur
you say

& I say there's
no hope
for the snowblind
eave wasps
who've stumbled out early

& thrash so
slower &
slower over the crust

till now they're
strangely
illuminated specks
of black

you'd swear vibrate

as the heavy
march clouds
slur by

& the sun
bites

The Sacrifice

Who says the cow
can't know the child
it nourishes? She sees
where you are dumb. She goes
& comes back satisfied
as the farmer finishes his pulling.

Do you think the pig doesn't grasp
the fork you lift?

Our friends the animals,
the plucky carrots
& beets, the secretive cabbages
forgive us, leading our blind hands
to the sacrifice

that will set them free.

The Coons

A four-year-old girl
drowned today in the pond.
Her mother fell on the bank
pounding the greasy water with
her fists. The mud specks
made her tears run brown
off her chin when two old men &
the paperboy took her home
to the trailer. You watched

from our window. When I came back
from the liquor store you said
we can't drink gin tonight.
I told you how coming round a curve
suddenly a raccoon mother & five
little ones, I locked the brakes & slid
watching as, one by one, quickening
their pace just slightly they
came into view to the right of the fender

up the ditch a few feet & turned
to sit in a row, all six of them
smiling.

To The Hum

When I speak, it's always
to you, the hum
between the kerchief mother wore
the chill October day
we buried the collie

& the blood-leaf reaching
for a strange numbness
the morning the furnace broke free

A chewed duck's wing
near the culvert at the edge
of the pond
        the sadness
of the bulging fontanels

These are your organs

I find them year by year, the pulse
of your form in each
takes me the spell of your single skin

all my life is here

THREE

New Poems

Extending Foreground

You stretch me back
from violet haze
rinsing the ridge west
of here, your hand
covering the depression
where I had propped my eyes
over a color

& on your fingernail
a tendril, slight curl
of black
it's flea shit
you say & flick
your finger toward the cat where surely
there's more

black fur
he is
yellow eyes
in this dark landscape
his limbs extend foreground
to purple tree-tips
where the last pink light is a doorway

Storms
for Lois

We've known the thin
laser-like power
of straw stalk
driving
through oak

& the light ripple
along the wing vanes
as the monarch butterfly stops
its clipped flutter
& settles

The Pothole Sonnet

So I said find a pothole
in the desert, Wyoming or
Utah will do, & scoop a handful
of what little moisture's left
in the mud—beetles

& larvae, you might get
a tiny shrimp, wriggling, or
a floppy tadpole skin
soft with digested organs

ready to be sucked. Even
the near-dry pothole
is a universe, writhing with sex
& vast space. Your eyes, my love,
are not clear pools.

Salmon Fishing, Boundary Bay

The salmon, waves of them, spilled
onto the deck, the worn wood
gray & glittering with sea slime & scales.

She looked down to the hold
where sunlight seemed an acid bath
scalding the life from them.

She turned to the one beside her, his face
a little slack with a silly grin —
So much dying, she said, so gorgeous & evil.

The Bobwhite

You are aware of the smell left
by a humid evening —
the atavism
of the lowlands.

Each oak along the creek-bed vibrates
with cicadas,
spheres of hazard pumping risk
toward morning.

The sheep coat the hill-stubble with wool fat
as they sigh in their sleep.

You have awakened before dawn & wonder
how it is to be male,
penis shrunk
to an acorn of fear.

Nearby a live bobwhite
is being eaten.

Seventeen Year Locust

To him the window
blurred with locusts
becomes a picture
of his infancy, a small room
writhing where his sister
has submerged him in the cold tub.

He is drowned. The locusts have darkened
the cellar. She hasn't
brought him food in four days
& now his appetite is gone.

Mom & Sally

You are seventeen, your name
is Sally & you
get wet
when you kiss your Mom.

For six years your sex life
has been a still
you've dabbed at but
never changed. There's no

blonde college boy who loves
the physical,
no shifty neighbor
who peeps while you read &

move your hand. There's just the two
of you, & the breathlessness
you live in
with the chickens, the cat,

the doberman & the bats in the barn.

December Thirteen

Today I saw a proud
teenage woman
bearing her load of pimples
through the park.

The engine died & as
my clumsy sedan
rolled to the curb,
she approached with
a piece of green twig she'd been holding.

I've carried this all afternoon
she said,

it's for you.

The Italians

The bamboo was slick
  with rainwater
    that noon in
the museum courtyard.

A firmness took your face
  each time you finished
    a smile —
it's what we've learned

of Art. You parted
  your knees beneath
    the wool blanket & I pulled
into you. We engaged

the engine of your Volvo
  in the Cascades —
    what a marvel. What
a marvelous world the mountains

in fog. In another life
  it seems you saw me
    across a canal & your mouth
opened. My limbs knew you

as I breathed &
leaned into a shop.

The Pleasure

I am the sand
dollar.
I touched
your elbow
on the beach that evening when
dry shore-weeds rustled
& you learned you loved her.

She's left you now &
you stand open
like a pomegranate gone
to seed.

I see these things.
I've become a pleasure
growing on
your arm,
& now you've begun
to notice.

The Teacher

The ocean was in the room
with him & he knew
nothing could harm his
simple plan. The sound was
a soft weeping & breath from
warm velvety nostrils
he would remember later as
the touch. He spoke a command
& listened was thankful &
was saved. Light came then
from the sliced orange & apple
bitten, light between the linen fibers
& from scissors open, window,
panel, brick. I know these as my own,
I can teach this.

Carnegie-Mellon Poetry

The Living and the Dead,
  Ann Hayes (1975)
In the Face of Descent,
  T. Alan Broughton (1975)
The Week the Dirigible Came,
  Jay Meek (1976)
Full of Lust and Good Usage,
  Stephen Dunn (1976)
*How I Escaped from the Labyrinth and
          Other Poems,*
  Philip Dacey (1977)
The Lady from the Dark Green Hills,
  Jim Hall (1977)
For Luck: Poems 1962-1977,
  H. L. Van Brunt (1977)
By the Wreckmaster's Cottage,
  Paula Rankin (1977)
New & Selected Poems,
  James Bertolino (1978)
The Sun Fetcher,
  Michael Dennis Browne (1978)